D1528137

A BEGINNERS GUIDE TO
GOOGLE DRIVE AND DOCs

Step-by-step practical instructions to Google Drive, Docs,
Sheets, Slides and Forms

ROBERT
WILLIAM

DEER PARK PUBLIC LIBRARY
44 LAKE AVENUE
DEER PARK, N.Y. 11729

Copyright

All rights reserved. No part of this publication **A Beginners Guide to Google Drive and Docs** may be reproduced, stored in a retrieval system or transmitted in any form or by any means, electronic, mechanical, photocopying, recording, and scanning without permission in writing by the author.

Printed in the United States of America
© 2020 by ROBERT WILLIAM

Table of Contents

Chapter 2 45

Google Docs Basics............................. 45

Chapter 3 58

Google Sheets and Google Forms 58

Chapter 5 109

Google Drawing, Google Sites and Offline Third-party Apps.................... 109

Why This Guide?

If you have been thinking of how to save your documents in cloud to access them anywhere in the world on any device, then Google Drive is a good choice. Google Drive also enables you to design your own website without coding and much more. However if you need a comprehensive and self-explanatory guide to walk you through the basics of Google Drive and Docs, this guide is the right choice for you. In this book, you will be taking through step-by-step practical instructions with over 100 screenshots on how to use Google Drive and other embedded applications in Google drive to enable you get the best of Google Drive. The book enables you to do it yourself.

Chapter 1

Introduction to Google Drive and Google Mobile Apps

Google Mobile Apps

Google Mobile Apps are applications developed and packaged by Google that help support functionality across various devices. These Google mobile Apps are made to provide different services needed for human sustainability. They are required in your devices for the utmost utilization of multiple tools, and most importantly, they work together seamlessly to ensure your devices provide you with excellent user service experience and comfort-ability. Some examples of Google mobile apps include You-Tube, Google Maps, Google Drive, Google Calendar, Google Hangouts, Google Keep, Google Voice, Gmail, Google Now etc. Our interest is limited to Google Drive, and I am going to teach you the basics of how to use Google Drive in this book. Hence you can quickly get the most out of Google Drive.

Why you should use Google Mobile Apps

Google has been able to package mobile applications with fantastic functionalities which help in various aspect of human endeavor. The Google mobile application is presently available for Androids, Nokia, Blackberry, window mobile, among others. You can enquire the goggle mobile apps supported by your phone by sending "m.google.com/search" through any browser from your phone. Aright choice his made by using goggle mobile apps based on its functionality which includes the following:

1. Search History: if you forget to bookmark a critical web site, through goggle History, your recent queries will be scanned for a march.

2. My Location: Google's location function helps track your location without any delay. My location helps to avoid the stress of typing your site every time you want a direction to a particular place.

3. Voice Search: Google provides an application that allows you to say your search request instead of typing keywords. Voice Search saves time and energy.

4. Contact Search: Google helps you to search your phone for needed contact from your list

of fabulous contact to save your precious time and energy.

What is Google Drive?

Goggle Drive is a great tool developed by Google that you can use to create and upload files to the cloud and access them anywhere easily on any device. Google Drive is used on both workstations and mobile devices. Google allows free storage space of 15GB for every user of Google Account to store their stuffing the cloud. Meanwhile, you can purchase more extra space outside your free space allocation.

To make use of Google Drive Application, you need to get a Google Account. So I am going to show you how to create a Google account. Just follow the steps, as explained in the section below, and you will be useful to create a Google Account for yourself.

How to set up a Google Account

A Google Account is a user account that enables access to certain online services. Google Account is also known as Gmail Account. To create a Google

Account, follow the following steps, as illustrated below.

- Lunch a browser from your device. Your browser could be Google Chrome, Opera Browser, Firefox, etc.

- Click on "Sign in" from the upper right corner of the window, as shown above.

❖ Click on create account

If you already have a Google account, then you can access the account by entering your username or Email or phone number and click next for further processes.

❖ Fill in the form

Enter your first name, your last name, your user-name, and provide your password twice as illustrated. Then you click next.

❖ Click next

Here you enter your phone number

❖ Click next

When you click next, Google will send a 6-digit verification code to your line.

❖ Enter the code

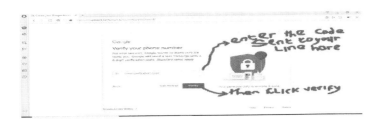

7

❖ Click "Verify"

❖ A Google Account is created.

How to Log in to your Google Account

Before accessing your Google Drive, you have to log into your Google Account through a browser. Meanwhile, Google Drive is best used with Google Chrome browser. To access your Google Account, follow the following processes and illustrations.

- Lunch a browser from your device
- Enter "gmail.com" in search bar and click on search

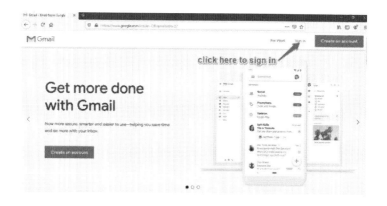

- Click on "sign in"as shown above

- Enter your "username/ email" as shown above
- Then, Click next

- Enter your password as shown above
- Click next

How to Access Google drive

Google Drive is one of the Google Mobile Apps which can be accessed through any device. To access your Google Drive, follow the following processes:

9

Method 1: Before login Google Account

If you have not logged in to your Google Account,

- Lunch a browser on your device
- Enter "google.drive.com" and search

- Click "sign-in" as shown above
- Enter your email
- Enter your password
- Click on the 9squares icon

- Click on "Google Drive"

Method 2:After log-in Google Account

If you have already logged in to your Google Account, then enter "drive.google.com"and search.

Navigating the main screen in Google Drive

To utilize Google Drive Application conveniently and comfortably, you need to understand the navigation of the features and tools on the main screen. The following clickable icons are found on the main screen of Google Drive, as shown in the figure below.

Search Drive

Search Drive is a search function that is to search for documents in your Drive. To search for a specific text/document, click on the search Drive, and open the folder of your interest.

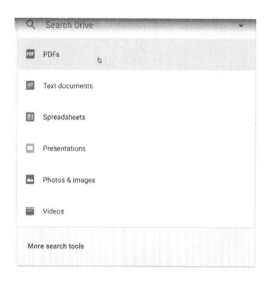

You can also search by using title. Here you enter the title of your file in search function and click on search as shown below.

Support

When you click on support, it will take you to Google Suite Learning Center. Google Suit Learning Center is a Google Drive Training and helps platform where you learn more about the use of Google Drive, and where you are provided with support based on your request.

Setting

You can view you drive storage capacity both used and unused. You can also buy more storage aside from the free 15GB storage allocated by Google, and you can see the items that are taking up the storage. You can also change the language, as shown below.

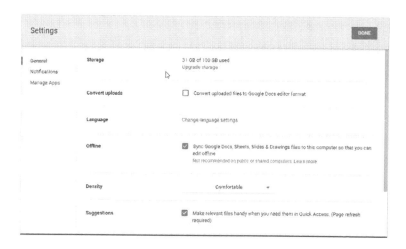

Through setting, uploaded files can be converted to Google Docs editor format. By clicking on Notification inside the setting, you can choose to get updates about Google Drive items in your browser likewise to get all updates about Google Drive items via email. It means you can get an email notification or browser notification. Besides, you can also manage other applications in your device. Here, you select the applications you intend to connect with Drive. You can add or remove Apps from within the Google Suite.

9 squares Icon

When you click on the 9 squares icon, you will be able to access Google drive and other Google Mobile Apps as shown below.

New

When you click on New, you will be able to:

- Create and re-name a new folder
- Upload folders
- Upload files
- Access Google Docs, Google Sheets, Google Slides, etc.
- Connect with more apps by using Google Drive

My Drive

My Drive is where there are folders and files that you have created or uploaded or shared with you. It is selected by default.

When you click on the dropdown triangle beside "My Drive," you will be able to execute the following tasks.

- Create a new folder
- Upload folders
- Upload files
- Access other features of Google like Google Docs, Google Sheets, and Google Slides, etc.
- Connect more apps to Google Drive

List View / Grid View

List view or grid view shows the arrangement of files and folders in Google Drive. You will click the icon to get different views. The list view shows the vertical arrangement of files and folders. Files and folders are arranged in rows and columns in the grid view. The figures below show the Grid view and list views.

List View

Grid View

Share with me

Share with me is a Google Drive feature that allows you to view all the files and folders other people share with you.

Trash

When you delete folders or files from your drive or when files are deleted automatically, they moved tom the trash until when you permanently delete them from the trash.

Backups

Backup is a feature that enables you to back up any files in your device such that you can fallback there to retrieve your stuff In case there is a problem with the device.

Recent

You can find files or folders you recently opened or edited or worked on in Google Drive.

Starred

Whenever you starred a file or folder, it goes into this place. You might want to star files or folders that are important or working on recently. Anything you starred would be seen easily. To achieve this, right-click on the file or folder. Then, select "Add to Starred" the dropdown menu.

Storage

Storage allows you to know how much you have used from your Google Drive Storage allocation and how the used spaces are shared across different applications in Google Drive.

What you can do with Google Drive

Google Drive is a powerful tool used to perform many tasks which include:

- Create files and folders
- Upload and store files and folders
- Download files
- Share and collaborate files
- Backup and Sync files, among others

How to create folder in Google Drive

You can create folder by using any of the following methods.

1. Create folder by using "New" button

   - Click on the "New" button on the left navigation menu just below the Google Drive logo
   - Select "Folder"
   - Rename the folder by entering your desired folder's name inside the dialog box containing "untitled folder" that popup

   - Click on "CREATE" button

2. Create folder by using "My Drive"

   - Click on "My Drive" in the left navigation menu
   - Right-click on the blue area
   - Click on "My Drive" from the dropdown list

- Click on " New Folder"

- Rename the folder by entering your desired
  name in the box that pop up

- Then, click on "CREATE"

3. Create a folder by Right-clicking on free white
   space on "My Drive" window as shown below.
   Then, Select "New folder."

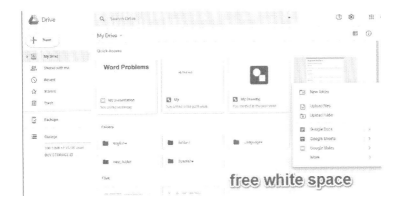

free white space

How to create file in Google Drive

Files can be created in Google Drive using some Applications, which include: Google Docs, Google Sheets, Google Slides, and more. There are many different ways to achieve this, which include: use of the "New "button, "My Drive" dropdown list, and "Right-click" whitespace.

By using the "New" button

When you have already logged in to your Goggle Account;

- Open Google Drive
- Click on "New"
- Select "Google Docs"/"Google Sheets"/"Google Slides"

23

- Click on "Blank document" / "From a template"
- Name the file.

By using "My Drive" dropdown list

- Click on "My Drive" in the left navigation menu
- Click on "My Drive" dropdown list just below the "search Drive box"
- Select "Google Docs"/ "Google Sheets"/ "Google Slides"
- Click on "Blank document"/ "From a template"
- Name the file.

By right-click on white space

- Right click the white space on your Drive window
- Then, Select "Google Docs"/ "Google Sheets"/ "Google Slides"
- Select "Google Docs"/"Google Sheets"/"Google Slides"
- Click on "Blank document"/"From a template".
- Name the file.

How to upload files or folders in Google Drive

In Google Drive, you can upload files and folders from any location in your computer to your Google Drive. When uploading a file or folder, the progress of uploading is shown at the lower right corner of the Google Drive window. When the uploading is complete, a message popup showing: "upload complete". To upload a file/folder in Google Drive, Follow the steps below.

- Sign into your Google Account
- Open Google Drive
- Click on New
- Select Upload file

- Select the location of the file in your Computer.
- Select the file.

- Then, click open

Note: You can also upload a file or folder by dragging the file from your desktop and drop it in your Google Drive. If you try to upload the same folder that already exists, a view option to tak popup, you may decide to cancel the upload process, keep the folders separately, or update the existing folder. If you are uploading an existing file, the case is a little bit different. You have the option to keep as a separate file.

How to download file in Google Drive

- Click on the file to highlight it
- Right-click on the highlighted file

- Select the "Download" button

- The downloaded file appears in your computer in Microsoft format.

file converted to excel

Share and Collaborate Files

In Google Drive, there are a few different ways by which you can share your files and folders. For example, you can click on the file or document and then click on the share button. Another way to do this is to right-click on the file. Then, select the share button. Also, you can open the file and then click on the share button.

All these different ways will take you to a common platform shown below. All these different ways will take you to a common platform shown below.

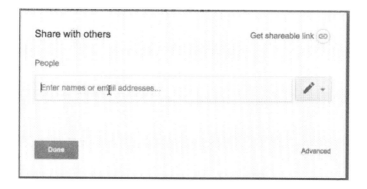

- Then enter their names/email address one after the other for multiple users.
- Select the permission action you want to grant the people you share the file with.

28

- Then, enter comment (optional)
- Click on "Done".

Searching For Files in Google Drive

Searching for files and documents in Google Drive is pretty straight forward.Click on the search drive

Enter the name/title of the file or a keyword in the file as shown below:

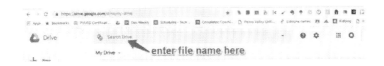

You can also click on the dropdown menu in the search Drive and fill some known information about the file as shown below.

Then click on "Search"

Backup and Sync in Google Drive

You can back up files on your computer so that you can have where to fall back to when your computer has a problem. To back up your files and documents in Google Drive, follow the steps below.

- Open your Google Drive
- Click on Settings from the top right corner of the window.

- Click on Download Backup and Sync for windows

- **Click on the Downloaded file to install the tool**

Thanks for downloading Backup
and Sync!

If your download does not begin, please click here to retry.

- **Open the tool**

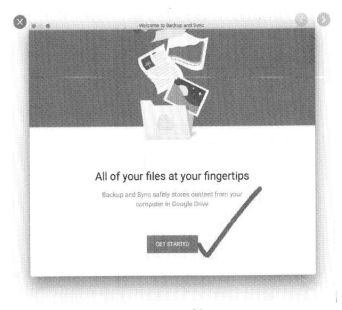

- Setup your Account to know the folders and files you want to backup and sync in your computer by clicking on "Get Started."

- Enter your password

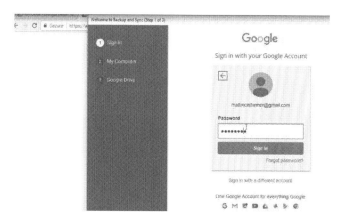

- Click on "Sign in"

- Click on "Got it" to specify the folders you want to backup from your computer

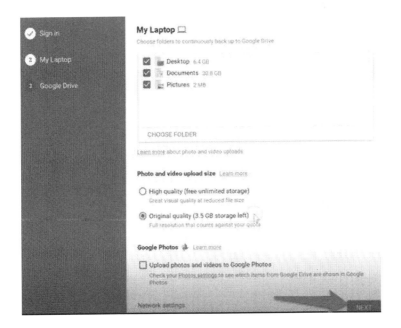

❖ Click on "NEXT" as shown above

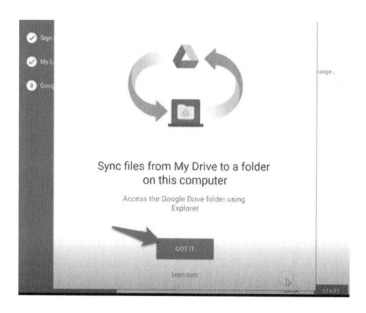

- Then, click on "GOTIT"

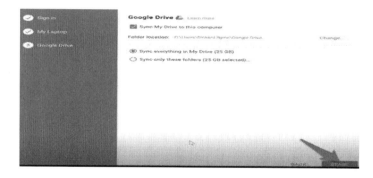

- Click on "START"

How to delete files or folders in Google Drive

There are different ways by which you can delete a file or folder in Google Drive. These include:

1. Select the file/folder and then select the "remove" button that pops up at the upper right corner of the Drive window.

2. Another way is to Right-click on the file /folder then select "Remove" from the drop-down list that popup.

3. Drag and Drop the file or folder in the "Trash" at the left navigation menu

4. Select the file or folder and press delete key on your device

How to delete files or folders from trash

When you delete a file or folder from the trash, then you are bound to lose the file or folder permanently. To do this, follow the steps below.

- Click on the "Trash" in the left pane menu on the Drive window

- Select the   file/folder you   want   to delete permanently
- Right-click on the blue line

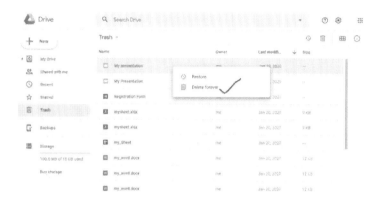

- Then, select "Delete forever"

Organizing the Google Drive

When you have many files and folders stored in your Google Drive, it may become very tough sometimes to know where exactly a particular file or folder is located. Therefore for effective searching and location of your files and folders, there is a need to organize your Google Drive. There are many ways by which you can organize all of your files and folders within Google Drive. I am going to expose five effective ways by which you can organize your Google Drive.

Upload selectively

When you upload so many files and folders in your Google Drive, there is every tendency that you upload duplicate files in your Google Drive. To reduce the accumulation of too many duplicate files, you should return on automatic file conversion by clicking on setting icon and select setting. Then select converts upload files to Google Docs. Then all Microsoft files that you have uploaded into your Drive to be automatically converted to Google Docs Editor Format, thereby preventing you from accumulating too many duplicates.

1. Organizing folders using Name.

When you are creating your folder, give names relevant to the content for a comfortable location.

You can create a folder where you store folders with relevant content.

For instance, in my Google Drive, I created a folder named Language, and I have two other folders named Spanish and English. I can move the two folders to Language by right-clicking on the folder and select move to and then click on "move."

before move

after move

2. Organizing folders Using Color

By default, the colors of folders are grey, which makes it difficult to quickly locate a particular folder from thousands of folders stored in Google Drive. Another way to organize Google Drive for easy identification of folders or files is by using a unique color for a particular set of a related folder. To change the color of a folder, right-click on the folder. Then, select change color and select the color preferred by extension. In my example Google Drive, I gave a unique color to Language, English, and Spanish folders, as shown below.

3. Organizing folders using "Emoji"

A visual creative of identifying folders and files can be achieved by adding emoji before or after the name of a folder or file. To achieve this, follow the steps below.

- Go to emojipedia.com
- Copy emoji of your choice
- Right-click on the folder in Google Drive
- Paste the emoji either before or after the folder's name
- Then, click on "OK".

Emoji is added to Language, Spanish and English folders in the Google Drive example below.

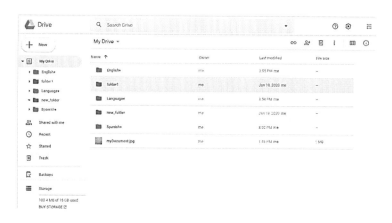

4. Update your view

You have two options on how to view the content of the Drive. Google Drive has the List view and the Grid

View. The contents are sorted by name by clicking on the arrow beside the name. The figures below show the shorting of List view by name in ascending order and descending order.

ascending Order

descending Order

One can also adjust the view by controlling the space density of the items as appear on the list. This is done by clicking on setting and selects the space density, which is comfortable, cozy or compact. Comfortable has an enormous gap, while compact is the most tightly packed.

Working with Microsoft Office Format

Google has made working in Google Suit with Microsoft office possible without having Office installed on your computer. There are features in Google Suit, which allows someone to perform the following tasks even though the system has Microsoft office. These tasks include: Add Office files to Drive, Open files in Drive, Share a copy of File in Office Format, convert Office files to Google files, Backup and Sync your files and folder.

How to add Office files to Drive

- Login to your Google Account
- Open Google Drive
- Click on "New"
- Click on "File Upload"
- Choose the Office file you intend to add

Open Office Files in Drive

This feature enables you to share office files with people who are not using Google Drive but only Microsoft Office. For Google Chrome Browser users, follow the steps below.

- Ensure Office Editing for Docs, Sheets, and Slides extension is not installed. To do this, follow the steps as follow.
  - Lunch Chrome Browser from your device
  - Click "More"
  - Click "More Tools"
  - Click "Extensions"
  - If Office Editing for Doc, Sheets, and Slides extension appears, Click Remove
- Open Drive
- Double-click on the Office file

Share a copy of file in Office Format

To share a Google File with people who only have Microsoft Office, it is required that a Microsoft copy of the file is attached to an email.

To do this, follow the steps below.

❖ Select the file in Docs,Sheets or Slides

❖ Click "Files"

❖ Select Email as attachment

❖ Select Microsoft Words, Microsoft Excel or Microsoft PowerPoint depends on the type of file

❖ Enter the Email address, subject and message

❖ Click "Send"

Convert Office Files to Google Files

If you and other people are working mainly in Google Docs, Google Sheets, or Google Slides, your office files, and PDF can be converted to Docs, Sheets, and Slides. This task can be done through the following steps:

- Login to your Google Account
- Open Drive
- Double-click on the Office file
- Click "File"
- Select Save as Google Docs/Google Sheets/- Google Slides depends on the file.

Chapter 2

Google Docs Basics

Google Docs

Google Doc is a free cloud-based application word document developed by Google. Google Doc can be used to create, upload, share and save files. It is similar to Microsoft word, where you type your documents, edit format, and save though Google Doc doesn't have the "save function" like Microsoft word. It has an automatic save. Once you create your document, and you name it, it automatically saves to Google Drive.

Google Doc shares some features with Microsoft word. It has a formatting toolbar where you can bold, italicize and underline a text. You can also change the color of a text. You can also change the font size of a text and equally change the line spacing. The formatting toolbar, the menu bar is almost the same as that of Microsoft word as shown below. Google Docs can be accessed anywhere on any browser through your Google Account.

How to use Google Doc

- Login to your Google Account
- Open your Google Drive by Click on 9 squares icon.
- Click on "New"
- Select Google Doc

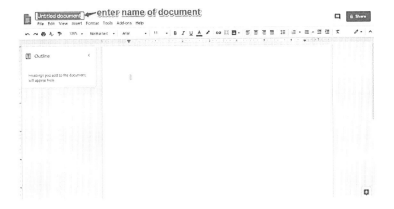

How to create a new document in Docs

- Click on "New"in Google Drive
- Selec Google Doc from the dropdown list
- Select "Blank Document" (or "Template" if you want to work with a particular template)

- Then click on Untitled document to name Doc

How to create a new document in a specific folder

You can decide to create a document in a specific folder location. As I am going to create a document named "my_Doc1" inside a folder named "folder1" just follow the steps below.

➤ Click On "folder1" which you want to create another one inside.

48

- Click on New

- Click on "Google Doc"

- Select Blank document

- Name your document

How to rename a new document in Docs

- Right-click on the document

- Select "Rename"

- Enter the new name

- Click on "OK"

Inserting images, page numbers in Google Doc

Adding images to a document is a great way to make the text elegant and attractive. You can add images from your computer, web, and Google Account.

Add image from your Computer

To add images stored in your computer, follow the steps and illustrations below.

- Place your cursor where you want the image to be on the document
- Click on the image menu on the toolbar
- Select "Upload from computer"

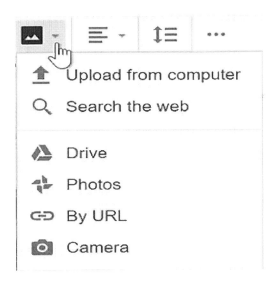

- Select the image you want

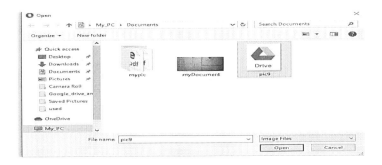

- Click on "Open"

How to add image from the Web

To add an image from the web, follow the steps and illustrations below:

- Click on the image menu on the toolbar
- Select "By URL"
- Enter the image address

- Click on "insert"

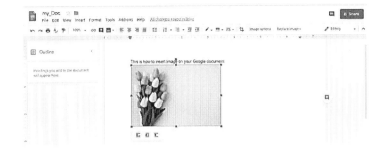

How to add image from your Google Account

If you have any Files or Folders in your Google Account, you can find these under Photo or Drive. These images include files and photos of other people shared with you. To add an image from your Google Drive, follow the steps below.

- Click on the image menu on the toolbar
- Select "My Drive" or "Photo"
- Select the image

- **Click on "INSERT"**

Import and Export Options

Files and folders can be imported into Google Drive by "drag and drop" method or using "New Menu" in Google Drive.

Drag and Drop Method

When you have your file in the desktop, click and drag the file from the desktop and drop it into your Google Drive window. You then receive a notification when the upload is completed.

Importing Using "New"

- Click on "New" in your Google Drive window
- Select "File upload"or " Folder upload"
- Select the location of the file
- Highlight the file to upload it from the browser window

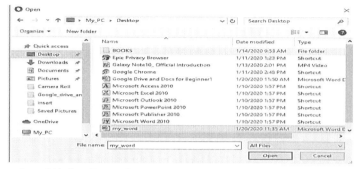

> Click "Open"

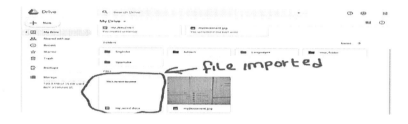

file imported

How to Open Imported File in Google Doc

To open the imported file in Google Doc format is pretty easy, just follow the steps below.

- Right-click on the file
- Select "Open with"
- Select "Google Docs"

How to export file in Google Doc

➢ Right-click on the file

➢ Select Downloads

➢ Double-click on the downloaded file to open it

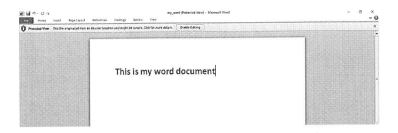

Chapter 3

Google Sheets and Google Forms

Google Sheet Basics

The Google Sheet is equivalent to excel in Microsoft word. To create a Google Sheet, follow the steps below.

- Click on "New" in Google Drive window
- Select Google Sheet
- Select Blank Document (or Template if you want to work with a existing template)

- Name the file created as indicated above

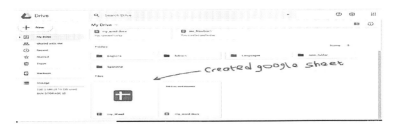

Import and Export Options

Spreadsheets files can be imported into Google Drive by the "Drag and Drop" method or by using "New" on the Menu bar in Google Drive.

Drag and Drop Method of importing files

When you have your spreadsheet in the desktop, click and drag the file from the desktop and drop it into your Google Drive window. You will then receive a notification message when the upload is completed.

How to Import by Using "New"

- Click on "New" in the Google Drive window
- Select "File upload" or "Folder upload"
- Select the location of the file.
- Highlight the file to upload it from the browser window

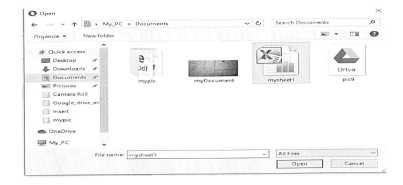

- Click on "Open"

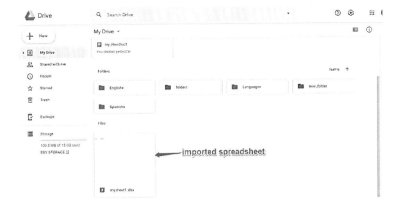

To open the imported spreadsheet file in Google sheet is pretty easy, just follow the steps below.

➢ Right-click on the file
➢ Select "Open with"
➢ Select "Google Sheet"

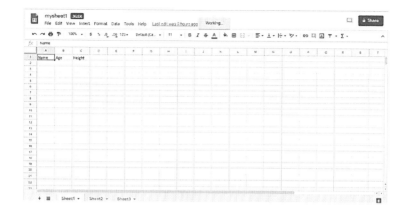

How to export file in Google Sheet

- Right-click on the file in Google Drive
- Select "Downloads"
- Double-click on the downloaded file Sheet to open it

Functions and Calculations

Functions are a great time-saving option for evaluating data in a spreadsheet. They can be used in place of formula when formula will be too long or too complicated. In the Google sheet, there are many inbuilt functions. To access these functions, click on the function command and a drop-down menu showing the inbuilt functions appears. When an appropriate function couldn't be found in the function command drop-down menu, then a user-defined function that suits the calculation is used. A function always starts with an equal sign. The function uses a specific syntax to include the name of the function, followed by one or more arguments inside the parentheses. The arguments give the values to be used during the calculation, as shown below.

In the function above, there is only one argument represented by a sub-range. A sub-range is expressed by two different cells with a column between them. The function above adds values from cellD3 through cellD12. To use more than one argument, we need to separate each argument with a comma. The following indicates a function with two arguments.

Consider a spreadsheet shown below.

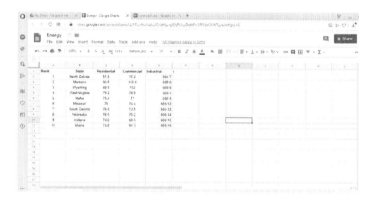

To find the total energy consumed by Residential

- Highlight the "Residential" column

- Click on the functions command. A drop-down menu which contains many functions as shown below.
- Select "SUM"

- Then, Click on "Enter"

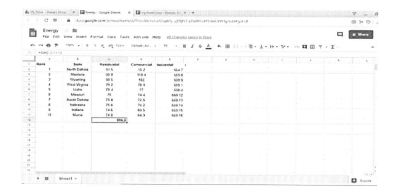

Using user-defined function

To calculate the total energy consumes by the ten states, the appropriate function to do this cannot be found in the function command. Therefore, you will design a user-defined function. To achieve this desired goal, follow the steps below.

➢ Enter the following function into the function bar.

= SUM (C2:C11, D2:D11, E2:E11)

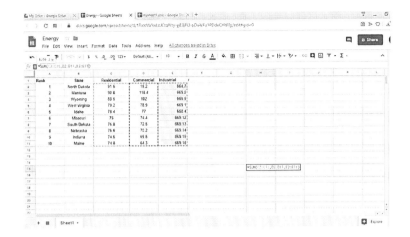

> Press "Enter"

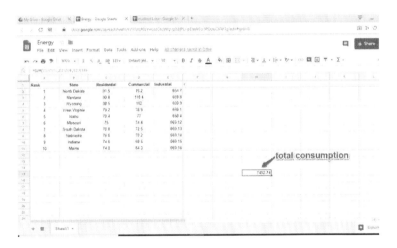

total consumption

Formatting numbers and Cells in Google Sheet

To format numbers, Google Sheet has some tools meant to carry out these tasks, which include: format currency, decrease decimal places, increase decimal places, and "more formats" through which other formats are selected.

To format dates, follow the steps below.

- Select the cell containing the date
- Click on "format" on the toolbar
- Select "Number" from the drop-down list
- Select your desired date format.

To format a cell, follow the steps below.

- Click on the cell that you intend to format
- Click on "Format" on the menu bar
- Select the type of format you want from the dropdown list

Charts and Graphs

Charts and graphs are statistical tools used for data analysis. When dealing with a chart or graph, it starts with the data. The data should be in a particular format that supports the desired type of chart or graph. We have single-dimensional data and multi-dimensional data. In single dimension data, we have an item against a unique value, while multiple values are associated with a single item in multifaceted data.

Single Dimension data

Fruit	Quantity
Orange	200
Banana	120
Strawberry	80

Multidimensional data

Fruit	Man	Woman
Orange	200	200
Banana	120	250
Strawberry	80	120
Mango	150	80

Google Sheet can be used to generate, Line chart, Pie chart, Bar Chart, Histogram, etc. To create a graph/chart in Google Sheet, follow the following general steps.

❖ Highlight the given data

fx	Atomic Number		
	A	B	C
1	Atomic Number	Atomic Mass	
2	20	40.2	
3	21	45.4	
4	22	47.8	
5	23	50.6	
6	24	52.2	
7	25	54.8	
8	26	55.9	
9	27	58.4	
10	28	60.2	
11	29	64.5	
12	30	66.9	
13			

❖ Click "insert" on the menu bar

❖ Select "Chart."

❖ Select the graph type(it may automatically generate a chat)

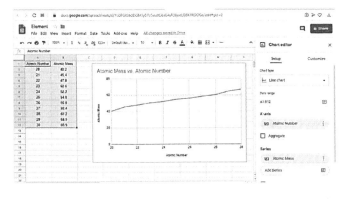

There is a chart editor which is used to customize the generated chart. Some of the tools that are used to customize graphs include:

Chart Style

Here, the background color, Font type and Chart border color can be changed.

To change the background color, click on background color. Then, select the color of your choice.

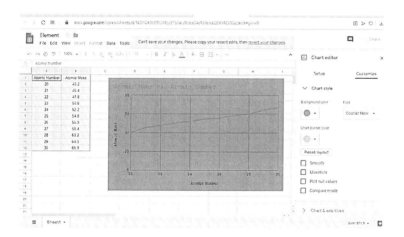

Chart Editor

You can customize the generated graph/chart through customized tab. Some of the tools used to perform this task are listed below.

Chart and Axis title

The following tools are available in chart and axis title.

1. Title type selector

Title type editor enables you to select the horizontal axis title, vertical axis title, Chart title and chart sub-title for editing.

2. Title text
   Title text contains the title of the features of the chart and which can be changed hereafter it has been selected.

3. Title font: The title font is used to select the individual font type of the titles.

4. Title size: Title size is used to select the individual font size the titles.

5. Title format: Title format is used to either bold or italicize the title text, and also to set the alignment to the left, center or right.

6. Title text color
   Title text color is used to choose a color for the title text

Title	Font	Format	Alignment	Color
Vertical Axis	Roboto	Bold		Red
Horizontal Axis	Georgia	Italic	Right	Yellow
Chart Title	Courier New	Bold	Center	Green

If the table above is used to customize the generated chart, the new look of the chart is given as follows.

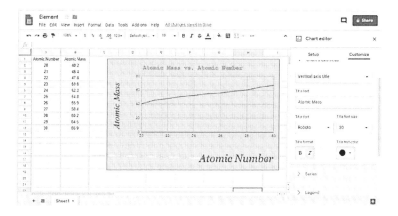

Series

Color: The color of the plotted points can be changed here.

Line dash type: The shape of the points is selected by using this tool.

Point size:The size of the point on the line is selected here.

Line thickness: Thickness of a line is selected by using the line thickness.

The above graph is customized by using the following table to give the next graph.

Line dash type	Dotted
Axis	Right
Line Thickness	4px
Point size	14px
Point Shape	Square

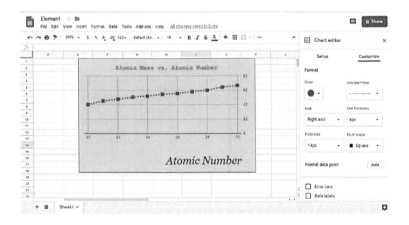

Column Chart

Add an element column to the previous data to suit for generating a bar chart. Follow the same process to generate a bar chart as shown below.

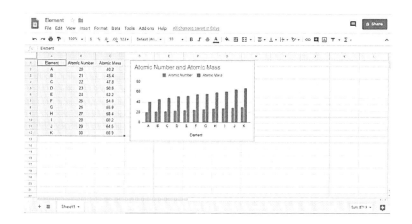

Share and protect your Google sheets

Google Sheet has features that enable users to share files with other people. It also allows desired authorization on the shared files. To share your file with other people,follow the steps below.

➢ Open the file
➢ Click on Share

➢ Enter "Email Address" of the person(s)

➢ Select Authorization status

➢ Then, click on "Done"

You can also share the file link and also determine the authorization to enable different access to the file. To share the file through "link", follow the steps below.

- Open the file
- Click on "Share"

- Click "copy the link icon"

- Select authorization status
- Enter the email address of the person
- Then, click on "Done"

Google Forms

A Google form is feature embedded in Google Drive, which can be used to get data from the users. Google form is used to create simple forms and complex forms. Google form can also connect with Goggle spreadsheets such that each time a user submits a form, the data is collected on the spreadsheet at the back end. The data that is collected at the backend is then used to generate a report, charts, or graphs.

Google form is used to get feedback from the audience, create a survey or poll among the targeted audience, and also to track the attendance performance in an organization.

How to create forms

- Login to your Google Account
- Open your Google Drive
- Click on "New"
- Click on "more" from the drop down menu
- Select "Google Forms"

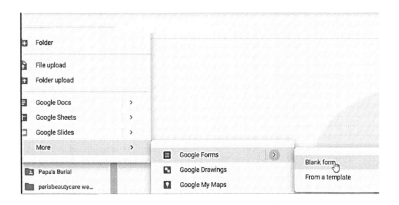

- Select "Blank form"(or "From a template" if you want a particular template)

- Name the form created

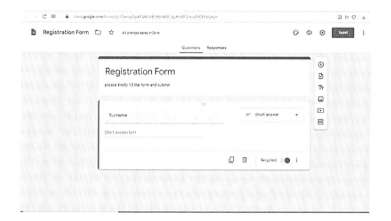

- Go back to your drive to view the form created.

79

How to Connect Form to Spread Sheet

A form is connected to a spreadsheet to collect data from users. The data collected in a spreadsheet format can then be used to generate charts. To achieve this, follow the few steps below.

- Open the form from your drive window
- Click on "Responses"

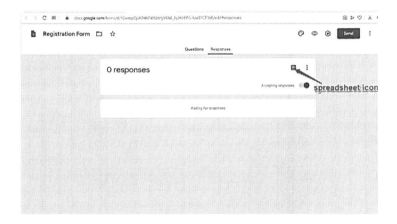

- Click on "Spreadsheet icon " as shown above
- Select "Create a new Spreadsheet"
- Select response destination
- Select "create a new spreadsheet"
- Click on "Create"

How to enter data and view responses

To enter user responses and view these responses in the spreadsheet, follow the steps below.

- Open the Form from the Google Drive window
- Click "Preview"

- Enter the responses to each question as shown above.
- Click on "Submit"

Registration Form

Your response has been recorded.

Submit another response

This content is neither created nor endorsed by Google. Report Abuse - Terms of Service - Privacy Policy

Google Forms

- Click on "submit another response" to enter another response as shown above.

- Click on "Submit"

- Then, open the spreadsheet from the Drive window to view the responses on the spreadsheet created.

Chapter 4

Google Slides Basic

Google Slides

Google Slide is a powerful tool embedded in the Google Drive service, and it is meant for giving presentations. It is a free web-based application that enables you to create, modify, and present dynamic slides. Similarly, Google's presentation can include animation, video, and much more. A slide show can be used to teach lessons in the classroom with text, graphics, animation, and even video. It helps to engage students in keeping lessons flowing while the teacher focuses on teaching. Google Slide has many tools and features that are used in the creation, customization, and handling of slides.

Navigating Google Slides Interface

Whenever you create a new presentation in Google Slides, the interface for Slide appears, as shown above. The interface is interactive, and through the interface, you can create slides, modify, choose the desired theme, play the presentation, and even share the presentation with others. Some of the features in the Google slides interface include:

The menu and shortcut toolbars

The Google Slides interface is incorporated with a traditional menu system with a shortcut toolbar furnished with different features and commands that enable you to work on your document.

The menu bar contains commands grouped by their functions which include:

- File: You can set up the page size using page setup; you can import slides, publish your presentation to the web, and share your presentation with other users. It also enables you to open a folder in your Drive to play a presentation, share presentations, create a new presentation, and rename your presentation.
- Slide: Slide enables you to create a new slide, duplicate already created Slide, and delete Slide. You can also use Slide to change the slide background as well as the theme.

- Insert: you can insert an image into your slides by uploading the picture from your device, search the web, Drive, or camera. You can also add text, video, audio, table, word art, and charts into your slides.
- Format: Format is used to customize text, tables, and images.
- View: View is used to play your presentation. This feature can also be used to zoom in and out of your presentation

The shortcut toolbar consists of buttons for some commands that are used frequently in the Google slides. The buttons in the shortcut toolbar include: background, layout, theme, Zoom and transition commands, among others. We also have "Share", and "Present"in the Google slides window.

Share allows you to collaborate with other Google Slides users. It also allows you to manage your sharing option. Present is used to play your presentation.

How to use Google Slides

The follow in general necessary steps that should be followed for easy use of the Google Slides:

- Create a presentation
- Edit and Format the presentation
- Share and Collaborate with other people.

How to create a presentation

- Login to your Google Account
- Open your Google Drive
- Click "New"from the Drive main window
- Select Google Slides

- Select Blank presentation

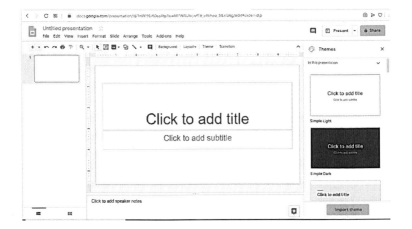

- Select a theme
- Rename the presentation

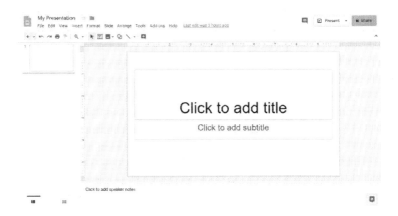

You can also create a presentation by:

- ❖ Login to your Google Account
- ❖ Enter "slides.google.com" in the search bar

Another way to create a new presentation is by URL: simply enter "https://slides.google.com/create" your search bar.

Add Text and picture to your Slide

❖ Click on the slide navigation pane to enter the title of the slide

❖ Click on "click to add subtitle" and delete if there is no subtitle

❖ Enter your text

Text can be entered in any of the placeholders on a slide. To do this, click on the placeholder. Then, type your text inside the insertion point that appears.

❖ Format your text by changing the color, font type,font size and more.

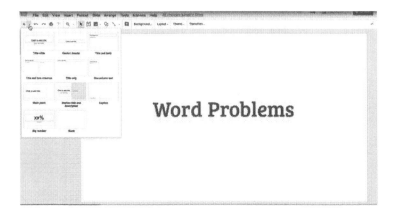

- Click on the dropdown menu beside "new slide icon" as shown above
- Enter the title and body of your content
- Insert an image by click on "insert" in the menu bar
- Mouse on image
- Select "Upload from Computer"
- Select the location of your image
- Select the image and then click on "Open."

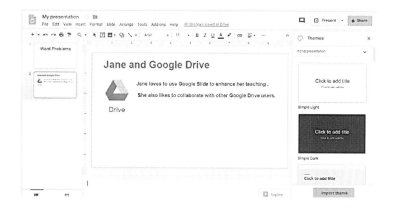

Editing features of Google Slide

Google Slide has rich features that are used to edit the content of your slides to make the presentation appealing. Some of these tools are shown in the figure below.

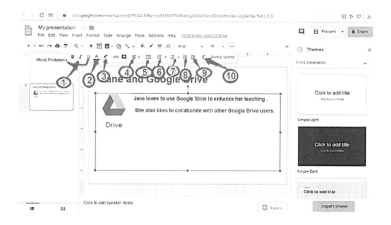

1. Text effect: Text effect is used to Bold Italicize or Underline your text

2. Text color: Text color is used to select your desired color for your text
3. Highlight color: Highlight color is used to select the highlight color for your test
4. Text alignment: Text alignment is used to define horizontal alignment (i.e. left, center or right) for your text
5. Line Spacing: Line spacing is used to define the spacing between your text lines.
6. Number List: Number list is used to give numbers list to your document
7. Bullet List: Bullet list is used to give numbers list to your document
8. Decrease Index: Decrease index is used to decrease your text indents
9. Increase Index: Increase index is used to decrease your text indents
10. Clear Formatting: Current text formatting is done by using clear formatting

How to enter text anywhere in a slide

Google Slides allow you to enter text anywhere you want in a slide. To do this, follow the steps below.

❖ Click the textbox command on the toolbar

❖ Click and drag to draw the textbox on the slide

❖ Click the textbox and type the text

Working with text in a slide

To work comfortably and effectively with a text in a slide, one should be able know how to **select text**, **copy and paste text** and **drag and drop text.**

Select Text

Click on the text areathen, highlight the text

Copy and Paste Text

❖ Select textbox

❖ Drag and drop the textbox where you want to paste the text

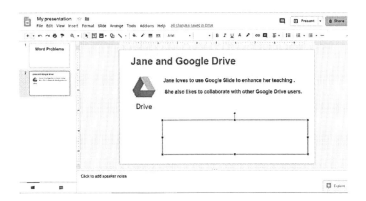

❖ Select the text >Click "Edit"on the menu bar

❖ Select Copy >Place the cursor inside the textbox

❖ Click on "Edit "on the menu bar > Select paste

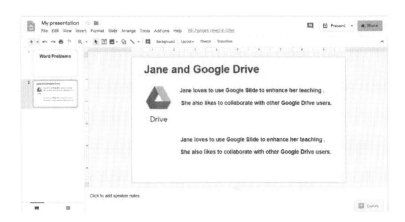

How to drag and drop text

❖ Select the text you intend to move
❖ Drag and Drop the text to the desired location

How to delete text

❖ Highlight the text
❖ Click "delete button" on the toolbar

Transition and Animation in Google slide

The Animation is making an object to move or fade on or out of the slide. Whenever animation is added to texts, images, slides, and other objects, some visual effects are created. Transition is the process whereby a slide changes to the next slide. Transition is an animation applied to the entire slide. For example, it could be set such that a slide is fading into the next one during the play of a presentation.

Google Slide has features that enable you to apply these effects to your slides to polish and make the presentation more appealing and attractive. There is an animation pane in Google Slide that allows you to decide the transition and animation configuration of the current slide.

How to add a transition to a slide

Every slide created has its transition default status as "no transition". Transition can be added to a slide through the following steps:

❖ Select the desired slide

❖ Click on "Transition" on the toolbar

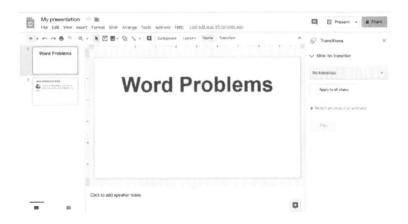

❖ An animation pane appears by the right side of the window

❖ Open the dropdown menu on the animation pane

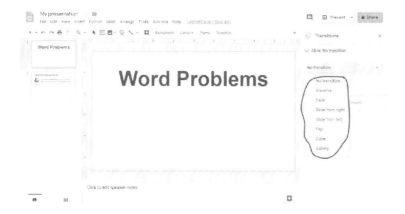

❖ Select your desired transition

❖ Adjust the transition speed to your taste. You can also set the transition for all the slides in the presentation as shown below.

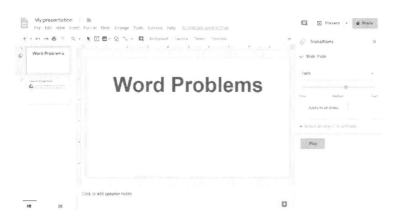

❖ The transition automatically saves into your presentation.

How to add an Animation

❖ Click on the desired slide in the slide pane at the left side of the presentation window

❖ Select the desired object by clicking on it

❖ Right-click on the object in the slide, then select "Animate" or Click on "+ Add animation" in the animation pane as shown below.

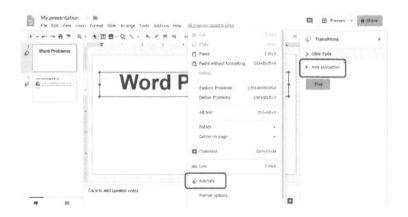

- ❖ Click on the first dropdown list and select your desired animation
- ❖ Click on the second dropdown list and select how to initiate the animation.
- ❖ Select your desired speed for the animated object through the speed control bar just below the second dropdown list.
- ❖ The animation is automatically saved against the object.

How to play a presentation

- ❖ Open your Google Drive
- ❖ Select the document by clicking on it
- ❖ Right-Click on the blue area
- ❖ Select "preview" from the dropdown list

❖ Click "play" from the new window

How to share presentation with others

Google has made provisions in Google Slide through which you can share your presentations with other Google Drive users. To use this feature, follow the steps below.

❖ Open your Google Drive

❖ Open your Google Sheet file

❖ Click on "Share" at the top right corner of the slide window

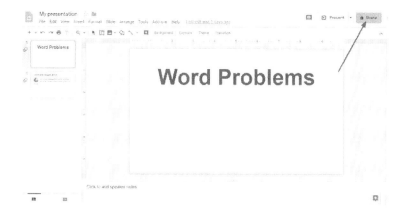

❖ Then, enter the names or email addresses of the people you want to share the presentation with

❖ Select the type of access you want to grant them by clicking on the arrow beside the pencil-like icon.

❖ Click on "Done"

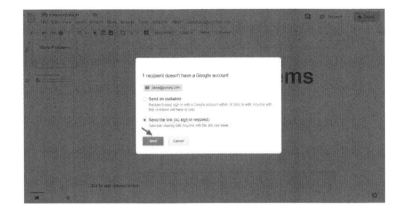

❖ Click "Done"

You can also share your presentations through a link by copy the link attached to the document and send to people through platforms like email, Facebook, twitter handle and more. To do this, follow the steps below.

❖ Open your   Google Drive   ＞   Open your
   Google Sheet file
❖ Click on "Share" at the top right corner of the slide
   window

❖ Click on "Advance" as shown above

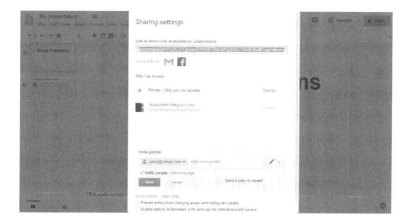

❖ Highlight the link

❖ Click on any platform (e.g. Mail)

❖ Enter the recipient email address and the subject

❖ Click on "send"

Online options using pull Everywhere

You can make your presentation available online for better collaboration. If you are using Google Chrome, you can go to the web store and add the extension "pollEverywhere" to your Chrome. To do this, follow the steps below.

❖ Login to Google chrome with your Google Account.

❖ Click on "Extensions" as shown above

❖ Enter "poll Everywhere" in the search bar
❖ Press "Enter"

❖ Click "Add to Chrome"

❖ Additional menu is added to the menu bar

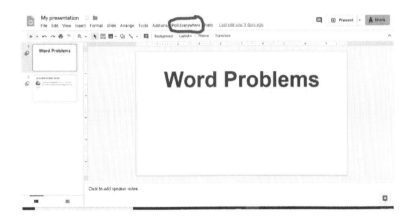

❖ Click on "polleverywhere " on the menu bar

❖ Mouse on the "New" from the dropdown list to create your poll

❖ Click Activity" to enable you to create your activities

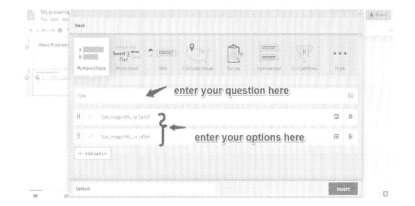

❖ Then, enter your question

❖ Click on "insert" to take it to your slide

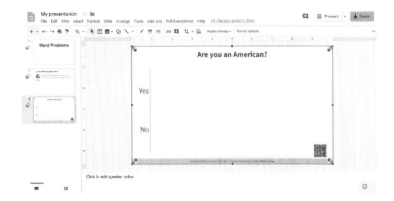

❖ Click on "present" at the top right corner of the slide window to play your presentation.

Chapter 5

Google Drawing, Google Sites and Offline Third-party Apps

What is Google Drawing?

Google Drawings is one of the great, free, and easy to use tools packaged in Google Drive that enables users to create their contents by drawing, inserting images, inserting text shapes, among others. It also allows users to create a diagram, flow charts, maps, and more. Its application is found in various fields like Mathematics, Sciences, Language Arts, and Social Sciences, etc. Anyone with Google Account can use Google Drawings freely and can also collaborate with other users on a particular drawing.

How to create a Google Drawing

- ❖ Login to your Google Account
- ❖ Click on the 9 squares icon
- ❖ Click on the Drive icon
- ❖ Click on the "New"
- ❖ Mouse over "more" from the dropdown list

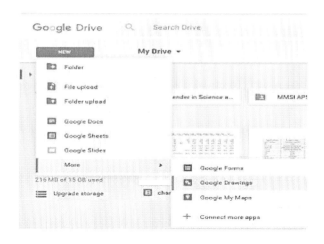

❖ Select "Google Drawings"

❖ Start to create your contents using the rich features in Google Drawing from the Google Drawing window shown above.

Navigating the Blank Drawing Canvas

The blank drawing canvas has the menu bar and the shortcut toolbar that contains different commands used in making your drawings. The menu bar is similar to the traditional menu function. It comprises of File, View, Edit, Insert, Format, and Arrange among others. The shortcut toolbar has the Select tool, Line tool, Shape tool, Text tool and Image tool, among others as shown below.

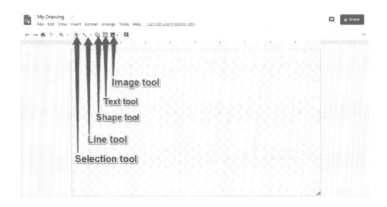

Format

The format is used to format a selected text, carry outline spacing, inserting bullets and numbering, add tables, change color and much more.

Arrange

Arrange is used to carry out the ordering of different object to determine which object is brought front. Grouping and ungrouping of objects are done by using "arrange."

Selection Tool

Selection tool enables you to select an object in the drawing. An object could be a single line segment, a shape or free picture and more. An object is selected by clicking on it. Whenever you select an object, a border containing small circles surrounds the object. The select button can also be used to delete any text, shape or objects you do not need. To do this;

❖ Click on the "select tool"

❖ Click on the object when the cursor changes to four arrows. Then, right-click and select "delete".

Line Tool

The line tool enables you to draw straight lines including an arrow, elbow connector, curved connector, curve, polyline and Scribble. To draw a straight line, follow the steps below.

• Click on the arrow besides the line tool

• In the drawing window, click and drag from where you want to start the line and release where you want to end the line.

Note: For a perfect straight line, hold down the shift key while you drag the mouse horizontally to get a perfect horizontal line or vertically to get a perfect vertical line. The scribble is used to make freehand drawing.

Text Tool

Text tool enables you to enter any text into your drawing. To enter text into your drawing, follow the steps below.

* Click on the text tool
* Click and drag on the drawing window to create a box on it
* Type your text inside the box
* Press enter to insert the text

Shape Tool

Shape tool is used to select different shapes, arrows, callouts and mathematical signs that best fit your drawing. To select a shape, click on the shape tool. Then, select your desired shape and drag your mouse to draw the shape within the drawing area.

Free Rotate Tool

Free rotate tool enables you to rotate any selected object to your desired angle. To do this, follow the steps below.

- Select the object
- Click and hold your cursor on the green circle
- Move the cursor towards left or right as you desired to rotate the object.

Color Fill Tool

Color fill tool enables you to select your desired color for any object. To do this, follow the steps below.

❖ Select the object
❖ Click on the color fill icon
❖ Click on your desired color for the object

How to create a Google Drawing

➢ Open your Google Drive
➢ Click on the "New"
➢ Mouse on "more"and Select Google Drawing
➢ Rename the file created by clicking on "untitled drawing"by the top left corner of the window.

How to change Drawing size

❖ Click on file on the menu bar

❖ Select "page setup"

❖ Adjust the size from the window that pop up

116

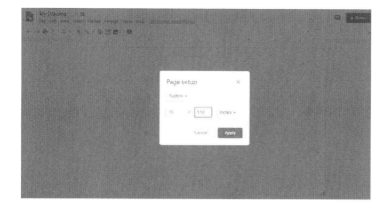

❖ Click "Apply"

How to upload image to drawing

❖ Open the   drawing document/create   a new drawing
❖ Click on " insert"on the menu bar
❖ Select the location of your image from the drop-down menu

❖ Select the image   and click "enter" (if uploading from your device)

How to add lines to drawing

❖ Click on "insert" on the menu bar

❖ Mouse on "Line icon"

❖ Select your desired type of lines

How to add text or Word Art

To insert text in your drawing:

❖ Open the drawing

❖ Click on "insert" on the menu

❖ Double-click on the drawing area to insert the box

❖ Double-click inside the box to insert the cursor

❖ Type your text

To insert WordArt

❖ Open the drawing
❖ Click on "insert"on the menu bar
❖ Click on "Word Art" from the dropdown list
❖ Type your text inside the window box that popup

❖ Press "enter"

The new Google sites

Google Site is a structural platform where tools are
available for you to create your webpages. The new

Google site is a new version of this platform where the creation of websites is much easier through drags and drop tools. It also makes collaboration much more comfortable.

How to create a Google Site

* ❖ Open your Google Drive
* ❖ Click on the "New"
* ❖ Mouse on "more"

* ❖ Click on "Google Sites"

❖ Rename your Google Site by clicking on "untitled site"at the top left corner of the window.

You can also create a new Google Site when you Enter "site.google.com/new" from search bar on your browser.

How to add your page title

❖ Mouse and Click on the page title box
❖ Highlight the text there and press "delete"

❖ Click the textbox to enter your page title

How to add more pages to your website

❖ Click on "pages" on the right hand pane in the Google Site window

❖ Click on "+" icon at the bottom right corner of the Window.

❖ Enter your page name in the box that popup

❖ Click on "Done"

How to insert "logo" to your site

❖ Click on the "Google Drawing name" at the top left corner of the site window

❖ Click on "Add logo"that popup

❖ Click on "upload"

❖ Locate the file where your logo is kept in your computer

❖ Select the logo

❖ Click on "open"

Accessing other Applications in Google Drive

Third-party sites and applications are created by application developers that are not Google. Google has made it possible to access other Apps that are not developed by Google from your Google Drive. To achieve this, follow the steps below.

❖ Open your Google Drive

❖ Click on the "New"

❖ Mouse on "more"from the dropdown list

❖ Select "Connect more app"

❖ Select your desired app from the list

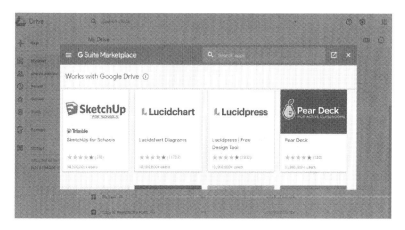

❖ Then, click on "install"

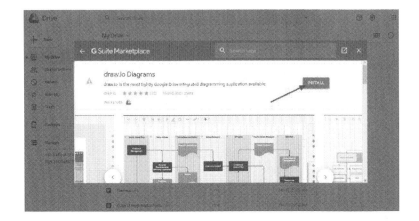

❖ Click "Continue" from the pop up box

❖ The Application is added to Google Drive

How to manage Applications with Google Drive

You can manage the application connected with your Google Drive to determine if they should be used by default or not. You may even decide to disconnect them from Google Drive. To do this, follow the steps below.

- Open your Drive
- Click on the "Setting" at the top right corner of the Google Drive window
- Click on "Setting" from the popup dropdown list
- Click on "manage Apps"

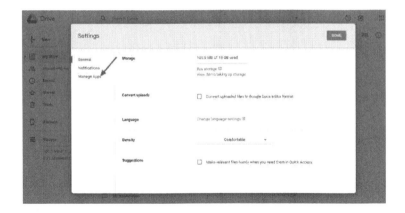

- Select your desired setting as shown above
- Click on "Done"

Chapter 6

Collaboration in Google Drive

What is Collaboration?

Collaboration is a process whereby two or more individuals or organizations work together to achieve a common goal. Collaboration is a feature in Google Drive, where you can share your files with other people, and everybody can drop their contributions by editing the document at the same time. You can monitor the progress of collaboration through file history. In file history, you can know who edited what in the file, and the contribution in the form of changes registered against their names.

Whenever you share a file, it makes it easier to collaborate on the document rather than sending different variations of the document back and forth through email. Everyone can work on the document at the same time. Students can collaborate on a group project work to achieve a common goal. Also, when companies collaborate, their teamwork together more efficiently, people get the right information at the right time, and collective knowledge they have gathered over the years to benefit the work.

How to collaborate a file in Google Drive

To work with other people in a document, you will share the file with them and permission is given to them to access the material. By default, when you newly create any document, it is not shared with anyone else. You are the only one who has access to the document.

There are three forms of permission you can grant to other collaborators on a particular file. These are view, comment and edit.

- View: Collaborator can only view the content of the file or folder but can neither comment nor edit it.
- Comment: Collaborator can view and comment on the document but cannot edit the content directly.
- Edit: Collaborators can view, comment and even edit the content of the file or folder directly.

How to share a file or folder for collaboration

Files and folders can be shared among collaborators to enable them share their experiences and expertise on the document at real-time. Sharing can be achieved by following the steps below.

- ❖ Open your Google Drive
- ❖ Right-click on the file or folder you want to share with people
- ❖ Select "Share" from the dropdown list
- ❖ Enter the email address of the person that you want to share with.
- ❖ Choose the access permission you wish to give them on the document

- ❖ Click on "send"

How to share a link to a file or folder for collaboration

❖ Open your Google Drive
❖ Right-click on the file or folder you intend to share with other collaborators
❖ Select "Share"
❖ Click "advance"
❖ Select the platform through which you intend to share the link (e.g. Gmail, Facebook, etc.)

❖ Enter the person email address

❖ Click on "send"
❖ Click on "done"

How to withdraw collaboration in Google Drive

Access permission granted to collaborators can be withdrawn such that they will not be able to collaborate. Follow the steps below.

❖ Open your Google Drive
❖ Select shared file or folder
❖ Click on "Share"
❖ Click on "Advanced"
❖ Click "Remove"next to the person you want to deny collaboration
❖ Click on "save changes"

How to remove a collaborator

To remove somebody from collaborating in a file or folder, follow the steps below.

❖ Open your Google Drive

❖ Click on the folder or file you intend to withdraw somebody's access

❖ Right-click on the blue line

❖ Select "share" from the dropdown list

❖ Click on "advanced"

❖ Click on the "*" sign next to the collaborator who you want to remove

Chapter 7

Google Drive Offline

Working Offline in Google Drive

Google Docs is a beautiful cloud-based processor that requires internet connections to make it work as brilliantly as it does. Meanwhile, Google makes provision for Google Docs, Google Sheets, Google Slides and more for users to be able to access their documents even when there was no internet connection. With Google Drive Offline, you can Edit, Create and save your document

To work with files and storage in Google Drive, be it Google Docs, Google Sheets or Google Slides, you need two things. These are Google Chrome and Google Chrome Offline extension.

There are two steps involved to set up Google Drive Offline.These are:

I.   Login to your Chrome Browser using your Google Account

II. Add Google Chrome Offline Extension to Google Chrome

How to sign in to Chrome Browser

❖ Launch Chrome Browser from your device

❖ Click the button with people at the top right corner

❖ Click on "sign into chrome"

❖ Enter your Google email and click on "Next"

❖ Enter your "password" and click on "Sign in"

How to add Google Chrome Offline Extension

❖ From a new tab Google Chrome, enter "Google Chrome Docs Offline Extension" in search box

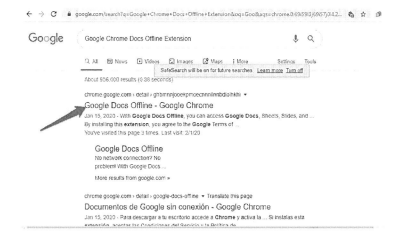

❖ Click on "Google Docs Offline-Google Chrome" as shown above.

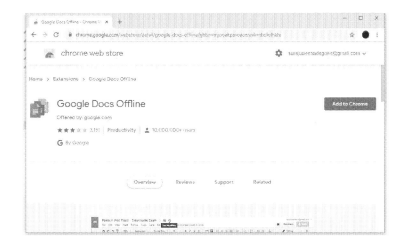

❖ Click on "Add to Chrome"

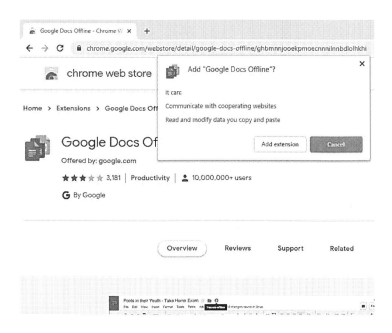

❖ Click on "Add extension"

Working with Offline files and Storage in Google Drive

You can access, edit and save your file offline. To do this, follow the steps below.

❖ Open your Google Drive from Google Chrome

❖ Click on "setting" at the top right corner of the Google Drive Window

❖ Click on "Setting" from the dropdown list that pop up as shown above.

❖ Enable the offline feature

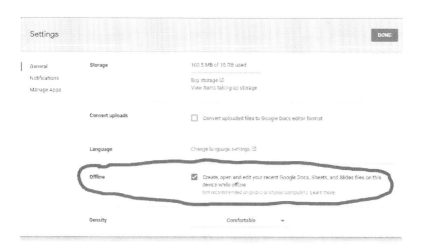

❖ Click on "Done"

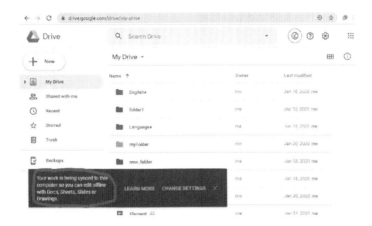

How to edit file Offline

- Disconnect the internet connection
- Right-click on the document
- Select"Open with" from the dropdown list
- Select the appropriate tool (Google Docs or Google Sheets or Google Slides) depend on the type of document
- Edit the document

Version history in Google Drive

Google version history enables you to review the previous versions of your document and let you graph that part of the text you have deleted but now found necessary or even restore the entire earlier version of your document. It is a convenient way to check the history of a document. If you made a mistake while updating a document, you could quickly go back to the previous version to recover the original text through version history.

How to check version history in Google Drive

- Open your Google Drive
- Select the document
- Open the document
- Click on "File" on the menu bar

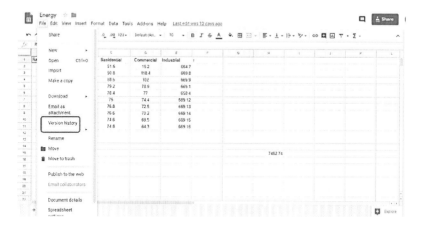

- Mouse on "Version history" from the dropdown list as shown above

- Select "See version History" as shown below

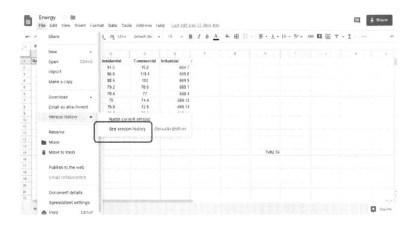

❖ Select to view or restore to any version of the document you want.

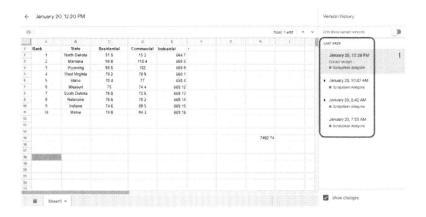

About the Author

Robert William is an information technology expert with over 15 years' experience in the ICT industry. He is an ardent follower of technological trends and personates in proffering solutions to complex problems. Robert holds a Bachelor and a Master's Degree in Computer Science and Information Communication Technology respectively from the MIT, Boston Massachusetts.

Made in the USA
Monee, IL
30 September 2020

RECEIVED OCT - - 2020

43636223R00090